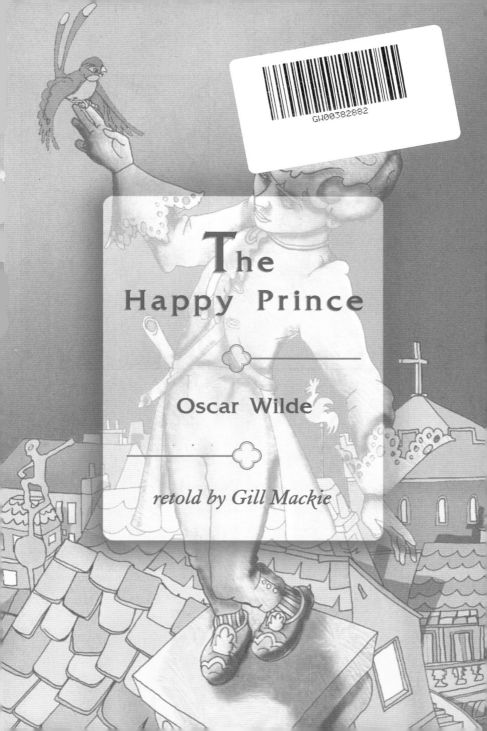

# The Happy Prince

Oscar Wilde

retold by Gill Mackie

# Credits

First published by New Editions 2000

Reprinted April 2006

New Editions
37 Bagley Wood Road
Kennington
Oxford OX1 5LY
England

New Editions
3 Theta Street
167 77 Hellinikon
Athens
Greece

Tel: (+30) 210 9883156  Fax: (+30) 210 9880223
E-mail: enquiries@new-editions.com
Web site: www.new-editions.com

Text, design and illustrations © New Editions 2000

ISBN  960-7609-81-6

Narrated by Tim Wilson
Recording and musical arrangements by George Flamouridis, GFS-PRO

Illustrations by Tim Wilson

Every effort has been made to trace copyright holders. If any have been inadvertently overlooked, the publishers will be pleased to make the necessary acknowledgements at the first opportunity.

# Contents

# Notes on the Series

## The value of reading

**New Editions Bestseller Readers** is a series of carefully chosen classical texts, retold by modern authors in such a way that students will automatically want to read more. The aim of the series is to encourage students of English to enjoy reading for pleasure, rather than just for study. Recent research emphasises the importance of reading in helping students to learn and develop vocabulary, as well as giving them a 'feel' for the language in terms of its syntax and modes of expression.

## The enjoyment factor

**New Editions Bestseller Readers** are illustrated, simplified readers that can be read in class or at home and have been carefully graded in terms of vocabulary, syntax, grammar and thematic content to meet the needs of students at each level. The books have been designed in such a way that students will be happy to read them because there are no signs of comprehension questions, exercises, etc. Instead, there is a simple glossary at the back of each book with an explanation in English of those words that may cause problems for some students and a separate activity book that provides students with an interesting way to understand and revise the story they are reading.

## What makes *New Editions Bestseller Readers* special?

They contain all the necessary ingredients students need to motivate them to read:
- attractive cover design
- modern, lively, full-colour illustrations, appropriate to each level
- interesting texts
- manageable amounts of text on each page
- separate activity books
- a cassette, recorded by professionals who really know how to tell a story

## Levels

There are six levels within a graded vocabulary range as shown:
- Level 1    300 words      Beginner
- Level 2    600 words      Elementary
- Level 3    1,100 words    Pre-intermediate
- Level 4    1,500 words    Intermediate
- Level 5    2,200 words    Upper Intermediate
- Level 6    3,000 words    Advanced

Students will be proud to be seen with a **New Editions Bestseller Reader**.

# Notes on the Author

Oscar Wilde was born in Dublin, Ireland in 1854. He attended Trinity College, Dublin and Magdalen College, Oxford. He published his first poems at his own expense in 1881. He got married in 1884, and had two sons, who were born in 1885 and 1886. Family life encouraged him to work, and he was the editor of the *Woman's World* from 1887 to 1889. He also wrote reviews for various journals at this time. In the period from 1887 to 1891, he wrote many of his short stories, including *The Happy Prince*. His only novel, *The Picture of Dorian Gray*, was published in 1891.

The beginning of a new period in Wilde's life was the success of *Lady Windermere's Fan* in 1892, and this success continued with his other social comedies *A Woman of No Importance* (1893), *An Ideal Husband* (1895), and *The Importance of Being Earnest* (1895).

However, this success proved to be shortlived, as Wilde was sentenced to two years in prison in 1895. His time there motivated him to write *The Ballad of Reading Gaol* (1898), and *De Profundis* (1905). When he was released from prison he moved to Europe, and died in Paris in 1900 at the age of 46.

His work, which has been made into ballets, a children's opera and films for both television and the cinema, has been translated into many languages and continues to be extremely popular today.

# Notes on the Story

*The Happy Prince*, which was published in 1888, is one of a collection of fairy tales which Wilde himself said were 'an attempt to mirror modern life in a form remote from reality — to deal with modern problems in a mode that is ideal and not imitative'.

The story is a simple one. The Happy Prince, as his name suggests, was a carefree prince who lived in a palace. When he died, however, he was made into a statue and put high up in a square. From there he can see all the poverty and unhappiness of the city, so when a little swallow comes to stay, the Happy Prince uses him to help the poor people in the city. Together, they do whatever they can to help, without thinking about their own well-being.

*The Happy Prince* is a well-loved fairy story. It has been made into a cartoon, and dramatised in a record by Bing Crosby and Orson Welles.

# The Happy Prince

Once upon a time there was a prince. He lived in the Happy Palace. He was very happy and the people in the palace called him the Happy Prince.

Many years passed and the Happy Prince became an old man. One day the old prince died and they made him into a statue. He stood in a square in the city. He was covered in gold, his eyes were two blue sapphires and there was a large red ruby on his sword.

One night at the end of summer a little swallow flew over the city. He was all alone. All the other swallows were in Egypt. You see, swallows always go to hot countries for the winter, but this little swallow stayed in England.

'I must find a place to sleep,' he said.

He looked for hours and he was very happy when he saw the statue of the Happy Prince.

'Oh, good! This will be my bed for tonight,' he said.

And he landed at the golden feet of the Happy Prince.

The little swallow was very tired. He put his head under his wing to go to sleep, but a large drop of water fell on him.

'That's strange,' he said. 'There aren't any clouds in the sky, but it's raining.' Another drop fell.

'I can't stay here. I must look for another place to stay.'

He looked up when he felt another drop and you'll never guess what the little swallow saw!

The eyes of the Happy Prince were full of tears. There were tears on his face. He was so sad and beautiful that the little swallow was sad, too.

'Who are you?' asked the little swallow.

'I am the Happy Prince,' the statue answered.

'But you aren't happy. You're crying,' said the little swallow.

'Up here,' said the statue, 'I can see all the sad and ugly things in the city. My heart is lead, but the things I see every day make me cry.'

'When I was a boy,' said the statue, 'I never cried. I lived in the Happy Palace. Every day I played with my friends in the palace garden and I never left the palace. I never went to the city. I was always happy and my friends called me the Happy Prince. When I died they made me into a statue and put me up here to see the city. Now I am sad, not happy.'

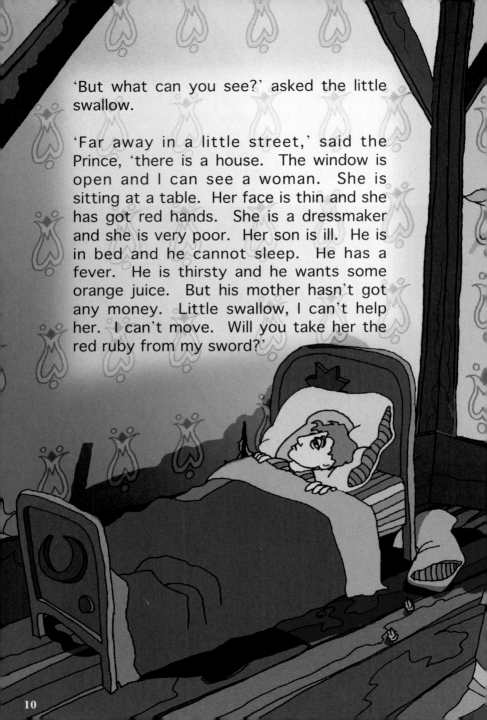

'But what can you see?' asked the little swallow.

'Far away in a little street,' said the Prince, 'there is a house. The window is open and I can see a woman. She is sitting at a table. Her face is thin and she has got red hands. She is a dressmaker and she is very poor. Her son is ill. He is in bed and he cannot sleep. He has a fever. He is thirsty and he wants some orange juice. But his mother hasn't got any money. Little swallow, I can't help her. I can't move. Will you take her the red ruby from my sword?'

'But I must leave,' said the little swallow. 'My friends are waiting for me in Egypt.'

'Please stay tonight and help me,' said the Prince. 'The boy is very ill and the woman is very sad.'

The little swallow didn't want to stay, but the Prince looked very sad. 'All right. I'll help you tonight. But I must leave tomorrow,' answered the little swallow.

The little swallow took the red ruby from the Prince's sword and flew to the poor woman's house. The woman was asleep in a chair next to the table in the room. There was a beautiful dress on the table. The boy was in bed, but he was not asleep. The little swallow saw that the boy was very ill. He put the red ruby on the table next to the dress. He flew to the bed and flew around the boy.

'I feel cool now,' said the boy. 'I am getting better.' And he fell asleep.

The little swallow flew back to the statue of the Happy Prince. He told him about the woman and the boy.

'Well done!' said the Happy Prince. 'Thank you.'

'Prince, I know it is very cold, but I feel warm now,' said the little swallow.

'You helped two people. It feels good,' answered the Happy Prince.

The little swallow thought about helping people and fell asleep.

The next day the little swallow was very happy.

'I'm leaving tonight. I'm going to Egypt,' he said. He flew all over the city and saw everything there was to see. In the evening he flew back to the square. He wanted to say goodbye to the Happy Prince. But the Happy Prince didn't want the swallow to go.

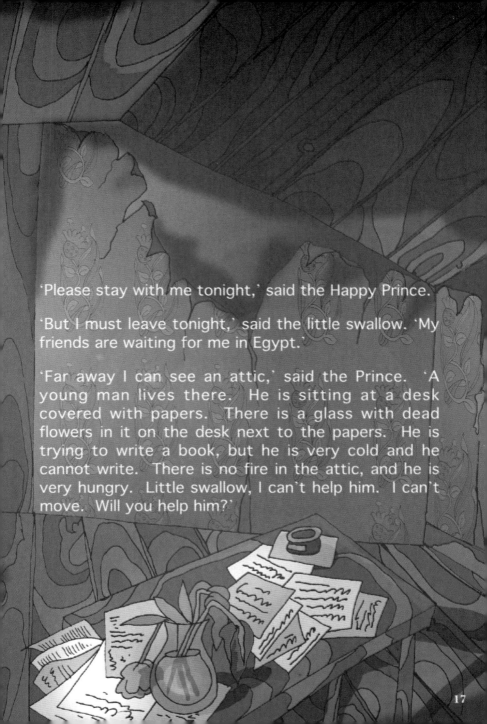

'Please stay with me tonight,' said the Happy Prince.

'But I must leave tonight,' said the little swallow. 'My friends are waiting for me in Egypt.'

'Far away I can see an attic,' said the Prince. 'A young man lives there. He is sitting at a desk covered with papers. There is a glass with dead flowers in it on the desk next to the papers. He is trying to write a book, but he is very cold and he cannot write. There is no fire in the attic, and he is very hungry. Little swallow, I can't help him. I can't move. Will you help him?'

'All right. I will stay tonight and help you, but I must leave tomorrow,' said the little swallow. 'Give me another red ruby.'

'I haven't got another red ruby,' said the Prince, 'but you can take one of my eyes. They are blue sapphires from India. They are a thousand years old. The writer can sell it and buy food and wood for his fire, and then he can finish his book.'

The little swallow didn't want to take the Happy Prince's eye, but the Prince asked him again.

'Please help the writer,' he said. 'He needs the sapphire.'

The little swallow took the sapphire and flew to the young man's attic. He was very sad. He had his head in his hands. He didn't see the little swallow and he didn't hear the little swallow's wings. When he stopped crying he looked up and saw the blue sapphire next to the dead flowers on the desk. He was very happy.

The little swallow flew back to the statue of the Happy
Prince.  He told him about the young man in the attic.

In the morning, the little swallow flew down to the harbour. He watched the sailors at work until it was time to go back and say goodbye to the Happy Prince.

'Please stay with me tonight,' said the Happy Prince.

'Winter is here,' answered the little swallow, 'and it is snowing. It is very warm in Egypt now. I must leave, Prince. I must. But when I come back next year I will bring you a present. I will bring you a red ruby and a blue sapphire.'

'In the square,' said the Happy Prince, 'there is a little match-girl. Her matches are on the road and they are all wet. She knows her father will be very angry with her, and she is crying. Give her my other sapphire, and her father won't be angry.'

The little swallow didn't want to take the Happy Prince's other sapphire. 'No, you will be blind!' shouted the little swallow.

'Please help the little match-girl. She needs the sapphire,' said the Happy Prince.

The little swallow took the Prince's sapphire and flew down into the square. He found the girl on the road. She was very sad. Her eyes were full of tears and she didn't see the little swallow. He put the sapphire in her hand.

'What's this?' she said. 'It's a beautiful stone! My father won't be angry now.'

She laughed and she ran home to her father.

The little swallow flew back to the statue of the Happy Prince. He told him about the little match-girl.

'I will never leave you now,' he said to the Happy Prince. 'You are blind now. I will stay with you forever.'

'No,' said the Prince. 'You must leave now. It is too cold.'

But the little swallow didn't listen to the Happy Prince and he fell asleep at his feet.

The next day the Happy Prince asked the little swallow
to fly over the city and tell him what he saw. So the
little swallow flew over the big city. He saw rich
people in their beautiful houses. He saw poor people
in the streets. He saw children who were hungry but
they didn't have any food. He saw children who were
cold but they didn't have a place to stay.

Night came and the little swallow went back to the Happy Prince. He told the Prince about the poor people in the city. He told him about the hungry children and the cold children.

'We can help them,' said the Prince. 'I am covered in gold. You must take it off, little by little, and give it to the poor people.'

The next day, the little swallow took some of the Happy Prince's gold. He gave it to a poor woman. Every day he took more gold and gave it to the poor people in the city.

One day there was no more gold. The Prince was now blind and grey, but the poor people were happy and the children had food to eat and somewhere to stay.

It snowed every day for a week and it was very cold. The little swallow was very very cold, but he did not leave the Prince. Then the little swallow thought, 'I am dying. I must say goodbye to the Happy Prince.'

'Goodbye, Prince,' he said.

'Oh. Are you going to Egypt?' said the Happy Prince. 'That's a good idea. It's very cold today.'

'I'm not going to Egypt,' answered the little swallow, 'I'm dying.'

He kissed the Prince and sat at his feet. He was dead. Suddenly there was a strange noise.

Craaaack! The Happy Prince's heart broke in two!

The next morning, the Mayor and his men were in the square. He looked up at the statue of the Happy Prince and said, 'Oh, no! The Happy Prince is very ugly. There is no ruby on his sword, he has no eyes and there is no gold. What happened to the gold? He is grey now!'

His men looked up at the statue.

'We can't have an ugly statue in our city,' said one of the Mayor's men. 'Take it down now! And throw away that dead bird!'

The same day, they pulled down the statue of the Happy Prince. They wanted to melt it and make a new statue, a statue of the Mayor, but the broken heart didn't melt. They threw it in the rubbish, next to the little swallow.

One day an angel flew down to the city. He asked all the people in the city for the two most precious things in the city. They all said the same thing: the Happy Prince and the little swallow.

'But I can't find the Happy Prince or the little swallow,' said the angel. 'In the square there is a new statue. It is not the Happy Prince. And it is winter. Where will I find a swallow?' he asked.

One of the Mayor's men said, 'We melted the statue of the Happy Prince, but his heart didn't melt. We threw it in the rubbish.'

The angel went to the rubbish and found the Happy Prince's broken heart. Next to it was the little swallow. He took them to God.

Today, the Happy Prince plays in the garden of Paradise and the little swallow sings by his side. The Prince and the swallow are happy again.

# Glossary

| | |
|---|---|
| alone (adj) | without other people |
| angry (adj) | the way you feel when somebody does something wrong or bad |
| another (det) | one more of the same thing |
| around (adv) | in a circle |
| attic (n) | a room at the top of a building |
| become (v) | start to be |
| blind (adj) | cannot see |
| cloud (n) | a white or grey thing in the sky where rain comes from |
| cover (v) | be on the top of |
| dead (adj) | not alive |
| die (v) | stop living |
| dressmaker (n) | a person who makes clothes |
| drop (n) | a very small ball of water |
| fall (v) | move to the ground |
| far (adv) | not near |
| feel (v) | be (feel hot, feel cold, etc.) |
| fever (n) | be very hot when you are not well |
| forever (adv) | always |
| full (adj) | have a lot of something in it |
| guess (v) | find the answer |
| harbour (n) | a place near the sea where boats and ships come and go |
| ill (adj) | not well |
| juice (n) | a fruit drink |

at

tail

t with

ur

touch someone with your lips
a grey metal
a girl who sells matches
the person who controls a town
heat something to make it like water
go to a new place, change position
after
sound

)

to

at a time in the past
go by
very special
with lots of money
the place where we put the things we
do not want
a red stone or jewel
a person who works on a boat or ship
a blue stone or jewel
give something to somebody for money
talk very loudly
the boy (child) of a man and woman
an open place in a town
something from stone or metal that
looks like a person
a small piece of rock
unusual

| | |
|---|---|
| suddenly (adv) | quickly and without knowing t[...] something will happen |
| swallow (n) | a kind of small bird with a lon[...] |
| sword (n) | a big, long knife that people fi[...] |
| tear (n) | drop of water that runs from [...] eyes when you cry |
| thirsty (adj) | want something to drink |
| thousand (det) | 1000 |
| throw away (phr v) | put something you don't want [...] the rubbish |
| tired (adj) | need sleep |
| tomorrow (n) | the day after today |
| ugly (adj) | not beautiful |
| warm (adj) | not too hot and not too cold |
| wet (adj) | with water |
| wing (n) | part of a bird's body which it us[...] |
| wood (n) | pieces of a tree which we use [...] make fires |